be Careful of what you Conjure (a short story)

By:Anthony Hawkins

ISBN:978-1-300-78539-2

Dedicated to the gay and lesbian community

Crystal was on her way to her bedroom,ready to lay herself to sleep in her huge queen size bed,just shrugging into her night clothes minutes ago.Crystal lived alone,tho she had a partner who visited her often,but she spent this night alone,only her and her empty and silent house.Crystal tied her long back length weave together into a scrunchy as she headed into her bedroom,rubbing facial cream onto her milky brown skin as she eased onto her bed,slowly pulling herself under her flower print covers.She then reached her hand towards her lamp,swiftly turning it off,her bedroom now dark.

Crystal closed her eyes slowly,but opened them after

only 10 minutes of keeping
them closed,unable to fall
asleep.Crystal pulled the cover
from her body and then headed
into her dark living area,where
she lit candles,and then pulled
out an old and wornout looking
weegie board from her hallway
closet,placing it on the
hardwood floor as the candles
still dimly lit her
surroundings.Crystal placed her

hands on the weegie board guider as she sat to the hard floor,and then began to chant and speak to herself,hoping something or someone would give her a sign.

Come on,do something,Crystal spoke silently,her eyes on the weegie board.Crystal wasn't into witch craft or voodoo,or any of those things,but she just played around with her weegie board every now and then for fun,something to do when she was bored out of her mind,and had nothing else to do.Crystal got no response from her weegie board,so decided to burn incenses,waving them around her house,hoping the incenses would add extra effect to her weegie board play,but the incenses did nothing,only giving the house a pleasant aroma.Crystal soon realized that her efforts in trying to contact spiritual forces or something otherworldly was failing,so she unfolded her legs and got to her knees,about to stand to her feet,but realized that the scented smoke from the incenses began to take a somewhat form,the form of a face,a smoky mist face.Crystal gave the smoky mist a glance,seeing that it closely resembled a persons face,but thought maybe it was just her imagination getting the best of her.

Crystal waved her hand through the smoke,causing it to fade,but the smoky mist gathered again,forming a somewhat smoky face again,a face that appeared more sinister and wicked rather than nice and friendly.Crystal's heart began to jump and her nerves rushed through her as she felt a quick and sharp feeling of fear jolt through her body,as she examined the smoky mist.Crystal felt cowardly at the fact that she actually began to think that the mist had a mind of it's own.Crystal had a quick flashback as she stood to her feet,a flashback of her deceased grandmother.

Baby the spiritual world aint nothing to be played wit,when you play wit them weegie boards and that other mess like that,you only inviting spirits and demonic thangs in ya house,stuff that aint of this world,stuff that aint holy,you betta start pleading the blood of jesus after you use that thing,Crystal's flashback of her grandmother played out in her head.

Crystal gave the smoke one more glance and then paused as the smoke began to slowly creep and float towards her.The smoke then sprayed into Crystal's face,as if someone had took a puff of a cigarette and blew it into her face themselves.Crystal began to choke out as the smoke filled her nostrils and lungs.Tho crystal was busy gagging and choking from the mist that blew into her face she could feel herself being lifted from her feet,now feeling her back against the wall.I been waiting for this bitch,a deep mans voice whispered to Crystal,tho she couldn't see who or what the voice belonged to.Crystal could feel something grip around her neck,as if someone was choking her,but whatever it was could not be seen.Dont act surprised broad,you been looking for shit,now you got it,the voice of a man spoke to Crystal again,as the invisible hands around her throat got tighter and tighter.Crystal had unknowingly contacted a spiritual entity,tho the spirit she contacted was not a spirit she was glad to see,but in her case,feel.

Crystal realized that the voice of the man and the smoky mist went hand and hand,the voice belonged to the mist that was now invisible and choking her to nearly death.Jes,Jes,Crystal choked out slowly,wanting to say the name Jesus,but could not fully pronounce it,still being choked by the wicked and invisible spiritual entity,an entity that was intent on killing her.Crystal began to struggle,tho knowing that she could not defend herself against the entity that held her by her throat,feeling she would die alone in her house,at the hands of an invisible being,a being she had no actual clue existed or where it came from,only knowing that she conjured it by fooling around with her weegie board,a board her grandmother warned her about years ago.Crystal could hear the entity snicker as her struggling began to come to a stop,her eyes shutting slowly.The smoky mist exited from Crystal's lungs as her movements became sluggish,it now outlined the structure of the invisible entitys tall shape and form,giving Crystal a slight glance of it's mass and shape.

Get the hell away from that child! A deep and powerful but feminine female voice spoke to the smoky mist as Crystal was about to take her last breath.The smoky mist fanned into the other direction by the command of the female voice,dropping Crystal from it's grip.Crystal deeply inhaled and then exhaled after being freed from the entitys hold,catching her breath again,previously feeling it about to slip from her lips.Crystal felt a warm presence surround her as the female voice whispered softly to her,tho she could not fully gather her thoughts to who or what the warm presence was,but knew that it had saved her from the clutches of the more wicked presence that still occupied the house.

Leave my granddaughter,i bind you,the female spirit spoke calmly as a strong gust of air blew towards the wicked invisible entity,causing the fire tips from the candles to flicker onto it,setting it on fire.The fire no longer lit the candles,but the wicked spirit instead.The wicked entity screamed a howling and deep echoing and pain filled sound as it twirled around the house blazing with fire,the fire now outlining and revealing the translucent wicked beings true form to

Crystal's eyes,the form of a man.The fire consumed spirit man exploded,leaving only smoke and dust behind.Crystal could hear the female voice blow air from her lips,causing the windows to crack and break as the smoky remains of the wicked spirit blew from out of the window,out of the house,as if it were being sucked or vacuumed out.

I love you baby,i see you again one day,one day baby,the soft and mature female voice whispered to Crystal before fleeing Crystal's presence.Crystal realized that once the womans voice left,so did the warm feeling she had.Crystal no longer had horror on her face but a slight smile,knowing who the female voice belonged to now.Grandma,i love you too grandma,Crystal whispered to herself,two tears slowly sliding down her face from her eyes.Crystal realized that her grandmother kept a protective watch on her even in death,or the so called afterlife.Crystal fell asleep that night,knowing that maybe,just maybe she

would see her grandmother
again someday.

Crystal threw out her weegie
board the next day,and then
grabbed her newspaper from
her porch,bringing it into the
house as she shut and locked
the front door behind
her.Crystal's eyes scanned the
newspaper,spotting a report of
an african american male

murderer and rapist that had died in an alley just the other night,after being stabbed by his female victim five times,just before he killed the victim herself.The man was wanted for six counts of rape and murder in the area,he had choked and strangled his recent victim to death,just as he did the others,but he had met the hands of death himself,at the hands of one of his own victims,very shortly after ending her.Crystal's eyes widened as she studied the newspaper,she realized that the same wicked spirit that tried to finish her,was the same man that finished the many victims who were described in the paper.Crystal quickly flung her newspaper into the trashcan,not reading the part where it said that the man had another male accomplice who assisted him on some occasions,tho the accomplices race and description was unidentified.

Crystal called over her girlfriend and partner of two years,telling her about her wild night,but making her think it was only a dream instead,thinking her girlfriend would think she was crazy if she told her the honest truth.Crystal's girlfriend just cracked jokes about Crystal's dream,not knowing that there was truth behind it,kissing Crystal until they both fell asleep.

A month had passed,and tho Crystal moved on with her everyday life,she still thought back to that day she was attacked by a spiritual being,not something you see on tv,but an actual spirit,a devious and wicked spirit,one that could have taken her life.Crystal cracked her front door as she bent down to reach for her newspaper,but jumped in fright as a tall caucasian man eased himself onto her front porch,now hovering above her,his eyes piercing and deep blue.Can i help you sir? Crystal questioned the mysterious man softly as she stood up again,now staring the man face to face.Yea,you got any sugar mam,i live just a few blocks down,im making brownies,meeting my girlfriends folks,wanna make a good impression,the man smiled at Crystal as Crystal smiled back.Oh,okay,just wait right here,i think i got some in my cabinet,Crystal smiled at the man as she shut and locked her front door,and then headed over to her cabinets,finding a small container of sugar,and then heading back towards the front door,reopening it.

Here you go,you can keep the container,Crystal smiled at the man as she handed him the container of sugar.The man eased the container of sugar out of Crystal's hand,and then gave her throat a glance,as if he was infatuated with it,his hands slightly twitching.Not to be a bother mam,but do you think i can have just a little more? The blue eyed man questioned Crystal,dragging the words out slowly.yea,no problem,just give me your container and i'll fill it up a little more,Crystal spoke to the man,trying to crack her door open just a little wider,so she could reach for the sugar container,but the door wouldn't budge,not a bit,as if something was trying to prevent it from fully opening.The man searched his surroundings and then moved a little closer to the door as

Crystal was trying and struggling to open it,but then realized Crystal's door was jammed,and couldn't fully open,just as Crystal did.

Damn,i think my door jammed,Crystal smiled at the man,still trying to budge the door,failing each time.Never mind mam,im pretty okay with this,see ya around,the man waved at Crystal as he exited from her porch,giving her and her neck one more blank and emotionless stare before heading down the street.Sorry about this! Crystal spoke to the man as he continued to ease down the street.Crystal's door finally swung open once the man was completely out of sight.A gust of wind gently hit and caressed Crystal on her cheek,a warm gust of wind,tho it was the middle of winter.Crystal flinched at the warm wind that touched her skin,but then turned her attention to her front door,wondering what could have caused it to jam.Crystal shut her door slowly and then locked it,and then sat herself down on her sofa,her legs crossed as she thought to herself.

Crystal reached for the picture of her grandmother that stood on the table inside a glass picture frame,and then began to examine it as tears splashed onto it.Crystal felt another warm feeling radiate over her body as she stared at the picture of her dead grandmother,the warmth made Crystal feel protected and loved.Crystal developed a new understanding of the world,all worlds,both living and dead,and realized that spirits did exist,both good and bad,and that her grandmother was one of the good ones.

The end

www.ingramcontent.com/pod-product-compliance
Lightning Source LLC
Chambersburg PA
CBHW050352290526
45785CB00006B/2741